AF471936

The Angels Who Saved Me

Mark Leyendecker

WestBow Press books may be ordered through booksellers or by contacting:

WestBow Press
A Division of Thomas Nelson
1663 Liberty Drive
Bloomington, IN 47403
www.westbowpress.com
1-(866) 928-1240

ISBN: 978-1-4497-8816-2 (sc)
ISBN: 978-1-4497-8815-5 (e)

Library of Congress Control Number: 2013904516

Printed in the United States of America

WestBow Press rev. date: 3/20/2013

Special Thanks

To my sister Maryann, who has helped me through this whole process. Without her, this might not have happened.

Thank you very much!

Love,
Mark

Table of Contents

Preface ix

Chapter 1 My Intuition 1
Chapter 2 The Doctor 5
Chapter 3 Our First Vacation 11
Chapter 4 Moments I Remember 15
Chapter 5 The Big Day 19
Chapter 6 The Angels Who Saved My Jennifer 23
Chapter 7 Sweet Sixteen 29
Chapter 8 The New Doctor and the Davy Jones Effect 33
Chapter 9 Jennifer's Story that Shocked Me 37
Chapter 10 Miss Independent 43
Chapter 11 As Life Goes On 47
Chapter 12 My Life with Jennifer 51

About the Author 55

Preface

This is a father's story about his daughter, who was diagnosed at birth with arthrogryposis and had to live all her life with hospitals and surgeries. After one surgery, while in the hospital, she died—not during surgery, but right before she was supposed to come home. Somebody slipped up, and she wasn't able to come home. This is the remarkable story of how the angels saved her and everything that happened—what she saw, what her father saw, what he found out years later from her story, and how it changed his life forever.

I would like to thank Jennifer's doctor, Dr. Sambhu Choudhury,
for his input and for being a great doctor to my Jennifer.

Thanks to my friend, Joe Morales,
for his work on my illustrations.
All illustrations due by Joe Morales.

Thanks Joe!

Chapter 1

My Intuition

It seems as though it was only yesterday that it was 1982. I was twenty-three years old and had been married for two years. My wife was twenty-one at the time. Our marriage was doing pretty well; we had our ups and downs like everybody else. We had jobs; she worked at a bank, and I worked in a machine shop.

As a kid, I always loved architecture, and I enjoyed building big tree houses with my friends. My passion was making plans and creating and designing homes. After I got out of high school, though, the last thing on my mind was more school. So I left town for about a year, just to explore our country a little.

At the same time, I had a girlfriend. I felt I needed to have this adventure, and I'm glad I did. After I got back, we stayed together, and a year and a half later, we got married. I decided to put myself through architectural school. As I was going to school, my wife got pregnant; we weren't ready yet, but hey, I was glad. I was going to be a daddy. At the same time, my third brother was also married, and his wife now knew we were pregnant. Wouldn't you know it—two months later, we found out she was pregnant, with a due date just one month apart from my wife's. This was good; our kids would grow up together.

Several months passed, and my mom wanted to have a birthday party at her house. So there I was, in the backyard of my mom's house, and my whole family was there—Mom, Dad, all eight of us kids, and my wife and sister-in-law. Everybody was having a great time. I was talking to my brother and just watching our two pregnant wives talking to each other, rubbing their bellies and smiling, and probably wishing their pregnancies were over—but just as proud as could be to be moms. And there was my dad, standing there with a glass of wine and a cigarette, as usual. He was very proud of his sons; he was smiling at us, knowing that we were going to make him a grandpa. He was also one of the proudest men I have ever met. Being a grandpa was tops for him, and we knew it.

My brother and I were both proud dads. We looked at our wives and said, "Yes, I did that." It's a proud time for a man. I was especially proud because this pregnancy had taken. We'd had four miscarriages before this one, so we took extra precautions and extra care of my wife to keep this pregnancy; with the doctor's help, everything was going well.

As my brother and I were talking, I happened to look over at Theresa. It felt as though things were in slow motion. As I stared at her for a minute, something hit me that I had ever felt before. This feeling I got was a very intense feeling that something was wrong. I tried to overlook it, but it wouldn't go away. I felt that the whole scenario was too good to be happening to me.

I just had to shake this feeling I had, but my gut, deep down, was telling me differently. I never told Theresa; I didn't want any more worries, so I just let it go. Theresa was due in two months, in September. My dad passed away six weeks before Jennifer's birth, one day before my baby sister's birthday. I grieved for the longest time. I was sad and mad at the same time. He never got to see his granddaughter or grandson.

A month passed quickly, and the time for the birth of my baby drew near. One day Theresa woke me at 4:00 a.m. and said those words: "It's time!" I got up, trying not to freak out, got in the car, and then realized I needed gas. (Hey, we weren't due yet!) Lucky for me, the station on the corner was open twenty-four hours. After pumping about ten dollars' worth, I heard her in the backseat of my Camaro: "Come on, my water broke!"

We left and hit the highway doing eighty. We got to the hospital and went in, and wouldn't you know it, there was nobody around. So I grabbed a wheelchair, rolled my wife in, and yelled, "Where is everybody?" Finally they showed up, acting all nonchalant. "Hey, it's my first child, and I'm twenty-three years old," I said. "I'm about to be a dad!" They put my wife on a gurney; she was breathing as she should. I was holding her hand and talking to her. "Everything is going to be all right; you're doing real good." The doctor showed up and, of course, took his time. I was nervous, and the baby was coming quickly. So as they were prepping my wife, I put a gown on. Yes, I went in with her; she needed me. Besides, I wanted to be there at my baby's birth.

I was so glad about becoming a dad; my thoughts of anything being wrong had left by this time. Did I mention her doctor had a beard and wore half-lens glasses down on his nose? We were about to deliver when he said, "I see her butt and not her head." He couldn't get the baby to turn around, so he said, "We have to do a C-section." I didn't think too much about this; it went pretty quickly. Jennifer was born at 6:55 a.m.; it took approximately four hours of labor. They put my baby on the scale and gave her a little spank, and then I heard a little whimper. Again, I still didn't think about anything being wrong. I saw my six-pound-four-ounce baby girl and couldn't believe it. I didn't see anything unusual.

We cried for that happy moment—I was a dad! While the staff was cleaning her up, I went to the restroom to change, all happy and giddy. *I have a baby girl who I love and will protect with my life*, I thought. Within minutes, the doctor walked in and changed my life forever. As I turned around to face him, he gave me a look of despair. Looking over his glasses, his bearded chin appeared to be dragging on the ground. He said to me, "Mark, we have a problem." My heart felt as if it stopped.

He didn't know what the problem was, nor could he tell me much. I ran to see my little girl and met up with Theresa. I could see some of the baby's physical characteristics. Her legs were still up. Now I knew why she hadn't been able to come out headfirst; she was a breech baby. Her feet and hands looked a little different, and her head was shaped like a football. I asked about that, and they said it was because she was born breech and that it would grow normally, and it did.

But she was so beautiful, with a head full of hair. They had to wrap her legs to keep her like that for a while. They put her in an incubator, and they rolled her up to our room so we could see her. Then they took her away to the hospital. So there was Theresa, lying in her room with a few other moms who had their babies to hold. We did not. I had never felt so bad for anyone as I did for Theresa at that moment, without her baby in her arms. We felt very alone and sad. We had been kids having a baby—and now we had a baby with problems.

I grew up that day. I knew we had more problems than I knew what to do with, but I had a beautiful baby girl who was going to need me more than ever. And I was going to be there, no matter what. Approximately two days later, we went to the hospital where Jennifer was, to meet the doctor who would take her case.

Chapter 2
The Doctor

When we got to the hospital, we had no idea what to expect. For two young kids like us, it was a little scary and intimidating, to say the least. We met the doctor for the first time. As he introduced himself to us, I found him a little intimidating and, as he talked a little, also arrogant. But he was one of the best for what Jennifer had. And later on I found we were lucky to have him. I wanted the best for my daughter.

Well, after about ten minutes of talking, he presented us with his conclusion. He said that Jennifer had a very rare condition; the odds of a child having it were approximately one in fifty thousand at that time. It was called arthrogryposis. We had no idea what that was, but he let us know. The next thing I remember is seeing Theresa go ballistic, throwing things, knocking things off tables, and crying out, while I stood there and listened to what he had to say. One of us had to keep it together. At this time, my heart was breaking into pieces. *My little girl has a problem.*

Theresa calmed down, and I have to give her credit; she accepted the news better than I ever did as time went on. Next, the doctor told us that she would go through many surgeries in her lifetime, and he was right.

> Arthrogryposis is a rare congenital disease that affects approximately one in three thousand live births. The cause for the disease process is not clearly understood, although there have been some genetic transmissions noted.

Some theorize that the problem comes from lack of motion of the baby as it develops in the uterus of the mother. The reasons for the lack of motion have been postulated to include decrease in the fluid around the baby, muscle and tendon development disorders, prenatal virus, and deformities of the uterus. Additional possible causes include the following:

- Dysfunction of the central nervous system such as spina bifida, brain, or spinal muscular atrophy
- Neuromuscular disorders such as myotonic dystrophy, myasthenia gravis, or multiple sclerosis
- Infections during pregnancy such as rubella or rubeola
- Hyperthermia of the fetus
- Maternal exposure to drugs, including alcohol and phenytoin (Dilantin)

Ultimately, regardless of the cause, what results is a baby that is born with multiple difficulties in moving. Fortunately, although some pulmonary and growth issues occur, there are usually no problems with language or cognition. This disease is discussed as being nonprogressive (i.e., the child does not worsen with age.

The child with arthrogryposis is born with very tight joints that make it difficult to move well. This tightness is sometimes associated with muscles that are also weak.

When issues associated with arthrogryposis are discovered in a child, several treatment options are presented to the family. Physical therapy is a mainstay of treatment throughout life, but in a baby, serial casting and surgical intervention allow improvement in range of motion as well as position of the joint for the maximum functional status. For example, an individual that cannot straighten out her elbow can be adjusted surgically through her bones so that the elbow is "unbent," allowing her to use her hand. Similarly, the feet of children with arthrogryposis oftentimes are rotated into deformed positions at birth, necessitating surgery to correct the abnormal position to allow for walking.

> Ultimately, as a child with arthrogryposis reaches adulthood, mobility and self-care are the greatest issues. Gait is usually unsteady if the patient is not completely limited to the use of a wheelchair. Some need caretakers or nursing facilities to allow for care of basic human needs.
>
> The path is often a long one for the family and the child involved. The rewards, however, are phenomenal in the understanding of the natural reserve and tenacity of these individuals. They are models for what humans can accomplish in life and should be considered heroes for what they show us is possible.
>
> Sambhu Choudhury, M.D.

While Jennifer was in the hospital, my mom came to see her, and we talked about what we were about to put Jennifer through in her lifetime. I didn't understand at the time, but Mom took it well, though she cried for me. You know, the more I looked at Jennifer, the more I felt in love with her. It became stronger every day. I was going to do whatever was necessary to make her life the best it could be.

I believe approximately one month went by before Jennifer's first surgery, which was on her legs. It breaks parents' hearts to watch their infant go through this. But it had to be done, and I knew she was in good hands.

Jennifer went through two surgeries, and then I got a call from my brother, who told me they had just had their baby boy. So I asked, "How is he"? My brother said, "Everything went well; healthy baby boy." So I congratulated him. A lot of things go through your mind in a matter of minutes during such times: anger, frustration, grief, despair.

I felt so bad for my baby girl. I felt that I had really let her down as a father, knowing that when she was growing up, she would know she was different and would ask a lot of questions. But at the time, she was an infant and I was still twenty-three with no answers yet. It was a sad time; my dad had just died and couldn't see his granddaughter. I hate to say this, but after Jennifer was born, I had to put my father's death out of my mind and concentrate on Jennifer and all we needed to do for her life.

Jennifer at age 3

Jen & Derick at age 4

Chapter 3

Our First Vacation

When Jennifer was three years old, she already had a number of surgeries under her belt. We had been free of any surgeries for a while, and I had just started my own design business in September. I started off with a great project, but we needed a break. So we went on a vacation for three weeks. We flew to St. Petersburg, Florida, where my mom had moved about a year before with her two younger brothers and sister. There were three things my mom had always wanted to achieve:

1. Have a large family (she did)
2. Live in Florida (she did)
3. (You will read later on in this story.)

We stayed with my mom for a couple of weeks, and we had a great time. But I wanted to do more, so we decided to go to Walt Disney World. Jennifer fell in love with it. She had just turned four, and she still remembers it. I carried her all over, and sometimes pushed her in a stroller. But what I remember most is when she hugged me and said, "Daddy, I love this so much, and I love you." It was the best day of her life. When we got back to Mom's place, our time was just about up. But before I left on vacation, I called a college buddy who lived in Colorado. He wanted me, my wife, and Jennifer to come out to see him and his wife and their five-year-old son. So we flew out the next day from Florida, with nice tans, to Colorado, where the air is a lot drier, as I found out. My skin started drying out. But they showed us all around. It was absolutely beautiful there, and we had a great time. Jennifer really liked their son; they became good friends. This buddy of mine is one of my best friends; he and his wife treated us so great while we stayed at their home. I thanked them from the bottom of my heart and then had to fly home.

A few years passed, and Jennifer went through more surgeries, therapies, casts, and doctor's visits. One of the worst parts of all this was that every time she went in, they needed to take blood. The infamous needles, the constant sticking—it wouldn't have been so bad if Jennifer had good veins, but she didn't. As a matter of fact, they could hardly ever find them, so it was one stick after another. This also went for all the IVs she had during surgeries. But as a last resort, they always found one in her neck. It was one of the most hurtful things I have ever had to watch. She tried so hard not to cry or whine. Sometimes I did the crying for her. She was such a brave girl, and we always told her that. The pain I felt watching my child going through this was intense.

It seemed that we were in hospitals half the time. The worst parts were when she was there from maybe two days to a week or longer. She always came home with some kind of cast on. I noticed she got bigger after some of the stays. (You might not believe that, but I had to carry her three-quarters of the time—believe me, I could tell.) Well, after we got back home after one of these hospital stays, I knew the inevitable was here. We finally broke down and got Jennifer her first wheelchair—an electric model. The doctor didn't think Jennifer was ready for that, but I said she was, and I was right. She didn't quite understand why she was in it, but she seemed to like it, and she learned very quickly how to drive it. The doctor was surprised she learned so fast, but I wasn't.

So a new chapter had started with her chair and us. I was hoping and praying that this would only be temporary, because we were praying she would start to walk soon. Our house was a few steps up, so I built a big deck and ramp for Jennifer and her new chair. It worked very nicely;

she loved it. Now she could get in and out of the house by herself. She was so proud of herself, and so was I. It meant a little more freedom for her, and she loved that. She also liked when people would stop over at the house, and they did frequently, including with my in-laws. One night, people were over and we were talking about Jennifer, and an older woman said one of the worst things a person can say: "I know what you are going through."

Well, needless to say, I snapped. She had no idea that the worst thing a person can say to somebody who has a child with problems is "I know what you're going through"—unless that person is actually going through the same exact thing. Later, I heard my father-in-law say, in a joking manner, "Don't you just love how everybody knows it all and tells you what they think you should do?" I was already bitter, and remarks like that, or worse, just made me more mad and bitter toward people at the time.

Chapter 4

Moments I Remember

It came time for Jennifer to go to school, and she couldn't wait. Boy, was I nervous, and it wasn't easy to get her started. I wanted to get her into a Catholic school, but none of them at the time were set up for her with ramps, bigger desks, or wheelchair-accessible bathrooms. So we had to put her in a public school, which turned out just fine. At first they weren't going to let her in because she was in a wheelchair; they wanted us to put her in a school for the mentally challenged, but my daughter was not mentally challenged. Also, this school was about thirty miles away. This was not going to happen.

We fought this and won. And it turned out they were wrong; my Jennifer was a B student. So everything worked out. Every year, they made sure she had what she needed, even when she had surgeries done each year and was out of school for a while, she always got caught up and always had good grades. I was so proud of her every day. Even the teachers loved having her around, and Jennifer made, and always had, friends. We were very glad for that, though we knew that if you met her, you could not help but love her. No matter what Jennifer had to go through, she never got mad or upset; she just knew that this was the way things were.

I, on the other hand, was upset for her, but I tried not to let her see it if at all possible. After going through this for a number of years, my wife and I started to learn how to deal with all our emotions. I have to hand it to Theresa, Jennifer's mom—she dealt with it better than I ever could. Sometimes I thought that deep down, Jennifer knew how I felt; I considered that that was why she always did so well with her circumstances. Feeling this way broke my heart even more than usual at times. I knew God had sent me an angel, and I was going to take care of her with every fiber of my being. (How could I not?)

Even when we went out to dinner, Jennifer never gave us any problems by screaming, crying, or just being a brat. I think this was because she just liked going out, enjoying Mom and Dad, the atmosphere, and the people around her.

When Jennifer was age four, we were sitting there enjoying our meal one night when some people came up and said, "In all the years we have been going out, we have never seen a more behaved and wonderful child." And Jennifer said, on the spur of the moment, "Thanks!" It was a funny moment I will never forget.

When she was age five, she was watching TV one afternoon, and something dumb was on. She turned to me and said, "What is this mess?" My jaw dropped; it was so hilarious.

Other moments stand out to me as well. One I remember happened when I lay down on the couch for a short afternoon nap. Jennifer rolled up to me in her chair and said, "Daddy, can I lay down with you?" Well, I loved that so much that it became our weekly ritual. It was the sweetest thing, and Jennifer still remembers that to this day. As a dad, I will never forget it. There are a lot of moments like this that I will never forget; they are wonderful memories.

Sometimes the memories are not so good. When Jennifer was seven, I was sleeping late at night when I heard a small, quiet voice through the monitor next to my bed: "Daddy, I had an accident." Well, I jumped up and went to her room. She started crying a little, maybe because she was scared or she thought she was in trouble because she had thrown up on herself. She had a bad migraine headache and she couldn't get up; she still couldn't walk.

I said to her, "Don't you worry about this," and I asked if she was all right. I said, "I've got you." First I wiped her face. Then I put her in a nice, warm bath and got her all cleaned up. I put new sheets on the bed, put new PJs on her, and gave her a couple of aspirin and some water. I then tucked her in, kissed her, and stayed there until she fell asleep, which was about five minutes later. As I was watching her, I realized how lucky I was to be her daddy, the daddy of an angel sent from God himself. As I went back to bed, I noticed Theresa was still sleeping and had missed everything. Well, almost—she would find the dirty sheets in the hamper the next day.

I remember one day when Jennifer was about six years old and in the hospital for an operation. She called me one day to talk. I was working, but I had to listen to her; she was feeling bad, and I guess lonely and a little scared. As I talked to her, I tried to keep her calm. I felt horrible for her, but I didn't know what to do, so I just kept talking to her. When she was finished, she kept telling me she couldn't hang up the phone because she couldn't reach it. So she laid the phone down and tried to call for a nurse. She thought I had hung up, but there was no way I was hanging up that phone. I felt so out of control listening to her cry in a whimpering way because nobody came to help with the phone. I kept calling for her, but she couldn't hear me. I couldn't stand it; I stayed on the open phone line for fifteen minutes, until somebody finally came in and hung the phone up. Then I left that instant to go see my Jennifer. It was heart-wrenching to hear that.

Chapter 5

The Big Day

By the time Jennifer was ten years old and had been through many surgeries, therapies, splints, and casts, it was time for a new wheelchair. I had finally realized by then that no matter what we did, Jennifer was never going to walk. So she got fitted for a new electric chair, with all the gadgets she wanted on it, to make her life as comfortable as possible. Even after all she had been through, she always maintained a "life is good" attitude. Sometimes I just didn't understand, but I loved her for that. It always seemed to make life just a little easier, especially after we found out about our next visit to the doctor's office. It was about Jennifer's spine. She also has scoliosis, which is a curvature of the spine, and it was getting near the time to have it corrected. Her age had to be between eleven and twelve years old, as that's when girls' torsos stop growing. Jennifer was about to embark on the biggest, longest, and hardest surgery yet. We had about one year for preparation.

There were times when I didn't know how much more I could take. As I watched my little girl going through this in her life, the worst was not knowing why she had to do so. Sometimes I thought, *God, will this ever end?* But I believe God has his reasons for all of us.

In prepping for the day of the operation, there were a lot of doctor visits to make sure she stayed healthy, and they explained a little more each time what the operation entailed. I don't think anyone can ever be ready for something like this. But I said that at Jennifer's birth, and we had made it so far. Sometimes I felt like a robot, just doing the steps and not always knowing why. But no matter how much I didn't understand or how much it hurt, we always did what we had to do. It was always best for Jennifer.

The day came to go to the hospital and check in. Jennifer was a little scared, of course, but as always, we talked like it was no big deal and we'd get right through it.

But I think Jennifer knew better. Even at these bad times, my little angel still showed all goodness and always stayed positive. I am a positive person and always have been, but this was beyond me. But again, I left it in God's hands.

After we checked in, the doctor came out and talked to us a bit, and then he took Jennifer to the operating room. We were by her side all the way to the "Not beyond this point" door. We all had tears in our eyes. I hated this more than anyone will ever know.

We knew this operation was going to be a long one; the doctor had given us an idea of that. But it was hour after hour of waiting and praying that everything would be all right. We stayed there all day, and finally, after ten long hours, the doctor came out to talk to us and describe what he had done. It was agonizing to hear, to say the least. He told us that even after ten hours of surgery, he couldn't do 100 percent of her spine. We asked why, and he said that to do the lowest section of her spine, he would have had to cut into her side, and he didn't think she would have made it, as she'd been out for a long time already. He wouldn't be able do it at a later time, because her spine was now fused to a pair of rods.

Let me explain the rods. There are two aluminum rods that are wired onto the spine, one on each side. After wiring these together, they fused the spine to the rods. The rods are bent at the end near the lower part of her spine. The idea behind this was that over the years, the bone would grow around the rods and straighten her spine, and it did. This is not the technical version, but it sums it up.

After this operation, Jennifer was in a body cast and had to stay in the hospital for two weeks, under numerous doctor's orders, the major order being "Do not put this child on her stomach."

So every day we would visit our baby girl. We often stayed for hours, and sometimes overnight. And each day, she got a little better. The body cast was a nuisance, but Jennifer tolerated it, as usual. Besides, it was not her first cast, though it was the biggest yet. We had a meeting the doctor the last night she was there, and he said she could go home the next day. We were so glad, and so was Jennifer. She was doing well and was ready to leave.

Well, the next morning, Jennifer called and said, "Daddy, I'm ready to come home, they said it's time." I said, "Great, honey, we are on our way." This was about 9:30 a.m. So we got dressed and left. I remember that morning in October of 1993; it was a cool, beautiful morning, and we were happy to go get our baby girl. Well, we must have left at the right time, as you will find out shortly.

Chapter 6

The Angels Who Saved My Jennifer

We got to the hospital within the hour; got into the elevator, and went to Jennifer's floor. When we exited the elevator and began walking to Jennifer's room, I noticed that the halls looked strangely empty, as they are sometimes depicted in movies. It looked like nobody was around, which seemed a little eerie, but I didn't give it a whole lot of thought. As we drew closer to her room, I looked around again and noticed that the hallways still looked empty.

When we arrived at Jennifer's room, there was a woman standing by the door as though she were guarding it for some reason. She had short, dark hair with gray around her temples, and she wore a long blue dress. She didn't move; she was very serene looking and very quiet. When I got to Jennifer's doorway, I said hi to the lady, and she turned to me and said, with a faint smile, "Everything will be fine. Jennifer will be okay; do not worry." I didn't give it much thought at the time, but it did seem a little odd. Just as I entered Jennifer's room, I noticed that the lights were out and it felt kind of cold. It gave me goose bumps. Still walking toward her, I noticed something eerie above her bed, though it was very faint. Again, I didn't give this a lot of thought because I was excited about getting my Jennifer. As I approached her bed, I called out her name two or three times because it looked like she was sleeping. Somebody had put Jennifer, in her body cast, on her stomach. As she lay there quiet, I rolled her over and called her name. Immediately I noticed a serious problem. Jennifer was purple, and blood and mucus were running out of her nose. She was limp. Jennifer was dead in my arms.

The view as I am walking towards Jennifer's room, and the Angel lady guarding her room.

From the look of her, I figured she had been out for approximately five to eight minutes. I quickly tried mouth-to-mouth, but it was not working.

I yelled for help several times. Code blue had been issued, but nobody had shown up yet; the lady who had been at the doorway was nowhere to be found; it was like she had just disappeared. The halls were long enough that I should have been able to see her walk away. I didn't give much thought to that at the time. The staff was soon running to Jennifer's room, with a priest in tow. There is nothing scarier than your child lying dead in front of you.

I watched in agony from the foot of the bed, gripping it tightly. I felt a few people trying to get me out of the room, but I wasn't budging. I tried to keep my mind focused to find out what was going on. As I was gripping the bed and watching people work on her, an odd thing happened. I saw an open grave right next to Jennifer, and I remember saying "No, you can't go yet. Please don't leave me. I love you so much. Please, God, don't take her." I kept repeating this over and over, and what I saw was astounding. I was watching this grave fill up with dirt. Once the grave was filled, green grass appeared over it with sunlight on it. The next thing I knew, I was in the hallway. I don't know how I got there. I noticed people around and Jennifer's mom crying with a priest comforting her. I started saying an abundance of words; I can't remember what I said, but my wife said to me later on I should have heard myself.

This all happened within minutes. I then heard my baby's voice, and I ran back in and grabbed her hand. She said to me, "Daddy, why am I back here; what did I do wrong now?" I broke down. I don't know how they brought her around—sticking her with needles, an oxygen mask, etc. I had never seen people so scared in my life. I mean, the looks on their faces—it seemed it took them forever to bring her back. But by the grace of God, she came back. They put Jennifer in intensive care for the next several days for observation.

As it turned out, Jennifer had suffocated on her pillow. With her head turned sideways at first, she got very uncomfortable, so she tried to turn to the other side but got stuck in the pillow. She tried to call for the nurse, but nobody was around. Although the call button was only two inches from her finger, she couldn't reach it.

The grave I saw from the foot of Jennifers bed, as I gripped tightly, asking "God, Please don't let her leave me!"

I called my family, and they were all there for me. With Jennifer being in intensive care, I had time to think about all this. I got very angry, as not one person came forward to explain, apologize, or comfort me in any way, not even her doctor. The more I think about it, the madder I get, even today. I understand this is hospital policy, as I found out later. But this doesn't excuse the fact that someone was negligent in his or her duties. They read the chart; they needed to follow it to the word, but they hadn't done so.

So if you put your child in a hospital, watch him or her closely. Read your child's chart; don't take anything for granted. The staff members are busy dealing with a lot of people.

Needless to say, I went to see a lawyer, the best in my city who took on malpractice lawsuits. I didn't want to, but they made me so mad by not saying anything to us that I felt I had to do something. I had to find out my rights, so I had a meeting with the lawyer, and he said he was sorry about the story. Then he asked me, "What is wrong with your daughter?" I asked him to explain, and he said, "Is there anything wrong with her that was caused by the incident, such as brain damage or anything at all?"

I thought about this for a minute and said, "Nothing is wrong with her." My Jennifer had been unconscious for approximately fifteen minutes, and nothing was wrong. They had tested her for everything, and the results were all fine. Then he said there was nothing he could do, and he was right: there was nothing anybody could do.

I had never felt so shunned in my life. But I had my daughter back and that was all that mattered to me. After a few weeks, I started talking to Sister Clarissa, a nun for many years—and my mother. (Yes, I said she was my mother.) I felt I needed to put things in perspective in order to understand them, because that's who I am; I needed to know. But my mother, being who she is, said, "Why try to understand it? It's God's way." After having a long conversation about all this, I finally came to my conclusion: I had my daughter back, and by a miracle of God, nothing more had happened to her. So I dropped my bad feelings and left it in God's hands. It was the best thing I could do. God sure does work in mysterious ways.

During all the surgeries after this one, you can bet we watched Jennifer closer than ever, and the hospital staff knew it.

Oh yeah, if you are wondering about my mom's third thing she wanted to do, that was to live the rest of her life as a nun. She had told me about this desire when I was a small boy, but I didn't understand, what with her being married with kids. After Dad died, there were no other men in Mom's life; she never remarried and never even had a boyfriend—my brothers and I might have had a problem with that if she had. After my baby sister turned eighteen, Mom gathered the family all around her and said to us, "I am leaving, and where I am going, you cannot come." She told us she wanted to live the rest of her life as a nun. We looked at each other in disbelief, but it was no surprise to us. Mom had been studying for it for years. Two weeks later, she left. She had known all along what she was going to do. It was sad for us at first, and it took us a long time to understand. I'm the oldest of eight children, and Jennifer is the oldest of seventeen grandchildren. Mom misses everybody immensely, and we do see her once a year. But twenty years have passed, and we are all used to it now. My mom not only devoted her early life to her family, but she also devoted the rest of her life to God.

Life throws us a lot of challenges every day. But my mom always said, "God doesn't give us more than we can handle." After Jennifer was born, I, as a kid at twenty-three, had the biggest challenge of my life, and I had no idea what I was going to do. I had many different feelings, good and bad, about what had happened to my Jennifer and the years that would follow. I was happy and angry at the same time and still not understanding what was going on. It took me years to get through a lot of issues about this, I am ashamed to say, because one never thinks anything like this could happen to one's own child. As a man and father like me, such things can be very difficult to accept. Then, when one thing after another happens constantly, you start thinking about God not giving you more than you can handle. So I found myself thinking, *How much can I handle year after year?* But the love I felt for my daughter was growing stronger and stronger. I never had any more children because I decided to devote my life to my Jennifer. She is my life.

Chapter 7

Sweet Sixteen

A few years passed since my mom left, and the surgeries subsided. Jennifer was doing well in school and had lots of friends. But now I had a new problem: all her friends were learning to drive. I had to figure how to get through this. I had known this day was coming. Of course, she heard all the other sixteen-year-olds bragging about going to driving school and getting their licenses. Finally, the day came when she asked me, "Daddy, is there any way I can learn how to drive?"

My heart was breaking again. Now I had to tell her the reality of her situation. There wasn't any way I could get her behind the wheel of a car. First, she was too short; she also didn't have the necessary muscle capacity in her arms or legs. I even looked into finding a vehicle that was made for people with conditions similar to hers, possibly one with buttons, but that wasn't available. We did look for some options out there, but in Jennifer's case, unfortunately, nothing was available. So I tried to let her down gently by letting her know driving is no big deal. I tried what I could, but Jennifer, being who she is, just said, "Dad, that's okay." I knew deep down she was hurt, and I hated that. But I did promise her that I would take her anywhere she wanted to go, wherever her friends were. And that wound up being okay with her, God love her.

When Jennifer turned sixteen, I made sure I did something special; I gave her a sweet-sixteen birthday party. I rented a big hall, and a client of mine at the time catered all the food and drinks for forty people at no charge; that was his birthday present to Jennifer. I was in a band at the time, and we played a live show for her. It was great day for Jennifer, with all her friends and family there, and it's a surprise she has never forgotten.

Jennifer was also becoming interested in boys at this time in her life. *Oh boy,* I thought, *something new I have to worry about as a dad.* But hey, I kept my mind open about this; even if only because I knew that if I didn't, she might never talk to me again. Soon I heard her ask, "Dad, can I go to the school dance?"

"By yourself?" I asked.

"No, I have a date."

"With a boy?"

"Of course," she said.

Okay Mark, stay calm, I thought. I asked her to tell me about it, and she did. I had promised her I would take her whenever she needed to go anywhere, and this went on until she got out of high school. I remember the first time I had to drop her off at the mall with her friends on a Saturday afternoon; it scared me to death. But her friends convinced me they would take good care of her, so I agreed. And when I picked her up later that day, everything was okay. Every time after that, I felt better about it, and the outings grew longer each time. Jennifer had good friends.

To most people, leaving your sixteen- or seventeen-year-old daughter at the mall may not be a big deal, but for me it was different. I tried not to let her see that when possible, especially when I had to take her to all the different places she wanted to go to with her friends. I wanted her to feel as normal as possible. But as you will read later on, this didn't get any easier.

Jennifer graduated high school, and I was very proud of her. She endured a lot of obstacles through the school years, but she never gave up, and she graduated as a B student. Her mom and I split up a few years before she graduated, and after her graduation, she came and lived with me. I bought us a house, and I fixed up a very nice bedroom for her. She loved it. I made it so she could have friends over and spend the night when they wanted. That's the way it happened a lot, because Jennifer couldn't spend the night at her friends' houses, as nobody could take care of her. She sometimes was sad about this, but she always understood.

Chapter 8

The New Doctor and the Davy Jones Effect

Jennifer was about to turn eighteen, and I knew this meant more changes were on the way. The first thing that would be changing was her doctor. Her orthopedic doctor saw children up to eighteen, but he saw Jennifer until she turned nineteen. We got a few names for new doctors to visit in order to tell them about Jennifer's condition and history, and just to get let them get to know Jennifer. I knew this wasn't going to be easy for Jennifer, as she was used to her former doctor. But we has known this day was coming for some time.

We started seeing the first doctor that had been recommended. We saw him a couple of times. But I always left it to Jennifer to see how she felt about someone; Jennifer had a good sense of people. The feeling wasn't there with this particular doctor. So we moved on to the next one; again, it didn't work out. I was not going to put just anybody with my daughter; it was going to take a special, caring, and compassionate doctor to take on Jennifer. Remember, this doctor would be seeing her for the rest of her life.

Another recommendation was made by her former doctor. We checked out this doctor's credentials, and then I took Jennifer to see him for the first time. Jennifer knew immediately that this doctor was the one, and I knew it too. I want to thank Dr. Sambhu Choudhury for coming into our lives—especially Jennifer's. He was exactly the doctor

Jennifer needed. He listened to her and cared about her like she was his own daughter. She loves him, even to this day. I knew she was in good hands with him, especially when it came to her surgeries—and there were a few coming up.

After a few visits with Dr. Choudhury, Jennifer began complaining about her hips hurting badly. I was always trying different movements and therapies on her to keep her from becoming too stiff. But after a doctor's visit and more X-rays, I found out she had arthritis on top of everything else, and the reason her hips hurting was that her leg-hip connection was bad. The ball of her joint was not round and smooth in the socket, as it should have been. The ball showed up as being more square than round. It was similar to making a fist and putting it in your other hand and moving it around without any sort of lubrication. You can see how this could be painful. I couldn't leave Jennifer in that pain. So we had to make a decision: keep her on heavy medication for pain, or schedule an operation. We made the decision to go ahead with an operation to remove the ball of her leg joint and have it disconnected. I'd never heard of this kind of operation, but all of her other operations had been new to me anyway. So we made arrangements for the operation. I knew she was in good hands with Dr. Choudhury.

Jennifer was about to turn eighteen, and I knew I needed to do something nice for her, though I wasn't sure what. I wanted to do something she would remember forever. I found out our city was having an Oktoberfest celebration over the weekend. This would have been good by itself, because Jennifer liked going into town, but there was a twist that Jennifer didn't know about. There was going to be a special person showing up downtown as part of a tour her was on to meet people and sell products. This gentleman had been around a long time, and I knew Jennifer absolutely loved him. So when I found out he would be coming here, that was it; she was going to meet the one and only Mr. Davy Jones of the Monkees.

I kept it a surprise until we got downtown; it worked out great. I planned it so we would be one of the last ones to see him so we could have more time with him, and it worked. When we got into the tent, there he was. The expression on Jennifer's face was priceless. She couldn't believe it, and we were the last ones to see him. If only you could have seen this. He was so good with her. Not only did he talk to her, but we also got pictures. He also gave her his e-mail and told her to write to him anytime. She got a kiss on her cheek from him as well; she blushed, but she loved it. We spent a good amount of time with him. I must say, he was a very nice man. I thank him from the bottom of my heart; he has no idea what he did for my Jennifer.

After we left, Jennifer looked at me and told me she loved me. She thanked me and told me it was the best birthday ever. I knew I had done well. Thank you, Mr. Davy Jones of the Monkees. I got one of the biggest hugs ever, but they are all good. Jennifer talked about meeting Davy Jones to everybody for the longest time. She was the envy of her friends.

Jennifer wanted to do more with her life. One day she asked me, "Dad, can I go to college?"

I said, "Sure." She was excited about this adventure. "What do you want to major in?" I asked.

She told me she wanted to do something with computers, computer programming, or something along those lines. Since I was computer illiterate, I didn't really understand, but I was excited for her and glad she wanted to have a goal. My Jennifer tried never to let her handicap get her down. She always wanted to do something for herself and try to stay busy, whether with her friends, her family, or just herself.

Soon thereafter, I took her to apply for college for the first time. I was there and had to be with her the whole time. It took a while, and there were a lot of papers to sign, but we got everything prepared for her.

Jennifer went to school for about six months and was loving it. I took her every day. I couldn't get a bus or any transportation without a major cost, but it didn't matter; Jennifer was happy to go, and so was I. But the excitement didn't last long, as Jennifer's hip began hurting so badly she couldn't take it anymore. I noticed it was hard for her to concentrate in school or on anything else. So we talked to Dr. Choudhury and scheduled her for a hip operation within a month. Jennifer had to drop out of school because of the operation. She was heartbroken because she loved school and had been doing so well.

When the time came for Jennifer's hip operation, she was a little nervous, but she was in good hands with Dr. Choudhury. He explained the operation to us. He would be taking her hip out, but he would not be replacing it. Why, you ask? Jennifer can't walk, so there was no reason to put a hip replacement in. Dr. Choudhury said that the operation would keep her from experiencing any more pain and keep her comfortable, and he was right. When I got her home after the operation, I kept her comfortable, and she healed up pretty quickly. With some therapy, she felt much better—until the other hip started giving her problems later on. But we dealt with that when the time came.

Chapter 9

Jennifer's Story that Shocked Me

After a short time had passed and Jennifer's hip had healed up, we were getting back on track, and Jennifer was feeling much better at this time. I got up one typical morning to cook breakfast and get Jennifer up and ready; little did I know that this was going to be anything but a typical morning. I was cooking in the kitchen when Jennifer wheeled in, looked at me, and said, "I have something to tell you, Dad." I had never before seen the look that was on her face, and what she told me astounded me. Breakfast was put on hold, as you might have guessed.

Jennifer couldn't hold it in any longer and felt she was ready to tell me. I had no idea what I was going to hear. She said, "Dad, do you remember the day I was in the hospital ten years ago for my surgery?"

"Yes, of course," I said.

"Here is what I didn't tell you."

"What is it?" I asked.

"When I was lying on my stomach, my head was turned sideways, but I got really uncomfortable, so I tried to turn my head the other way, but I got stuck in my pillow and couldn't turn around. I kept trying to call for a nurse, but no one heard me. I couldn't breathe, and I couldn't reach the call button. The next thing I remember is falling asleep, or that's what I thought, but I couldn't breathe."

My heart was breaking as I listened to this story. But what she told me after that shook my world to the core. I asked, "Did something happen"?

"After I passed out, the most wonderful thing happened to me. I saw this really blue sky with angels all around me. It was so peaceful, like never before. I thought I was having a special dream. Two special angels were holding me; they were so beautiful. They just kept holding me and saying to me, 'You are going to be all right.' I asked them, 'What happened, did I die?' But they kept saying, 'You will be all right; you are going back, because this is not your time yet.' But as I was looking at you, I saw an open grave next to me. I asked if it was mine, and they said, 'No, it's not your time yet.' I felt so good; there was no pain, and I felt so at peace. My body didn't hurt anymore. I felt I could walk. I felt so safe and warm. I didn't know what was happening to me, but I felt so good. I was not sure I wanted to go back. One of the angels said, 'The doctors are going to bring you back so you can be with your dad and mom.' Then they each said, 'We love you, child.' They flew away, and when they did, I woke up with doctors all around me; I was crying for you, back in the hospital bed. I was so glad to see you there next to me when I woke up."

I said to her, "Where else would I be? I will always be by your side."

Needless to say, I was astounded at what I had heard. You hardly ever hear stories like this; you're never sure what to believe. But when it happens to you, it changes your life forever, I promise. And for this to happen to my daughter is a godsend. Not that I am glad that my child went through this trauma, but something amazing has happened to my daughter, and I feel blessed for her.

I asked Jennifer many questions about this. Then I asked her, "Why did you wait so long to tell me?"

She said, "I just didn't think anybody would believe me, and I didn't know what to say." Jennifer had waited ten years for that day, and she had never told anybody else.

The angels said, "This is not your time."

After hearing Jennifer's story, it became very clear to me what had been bothering me all these years. The lady at her doorway was an angel guarding my Jennifer; she was there to let me know Jennifer would be okay. As I explained earlier, when I turned around, she was gone, and the halls were long enough that I would have seen her walk away. This also explains to me Jennifer's room being so cold, and the eerie appearance of her room that I had noticed but had never given much thought to. And what really got me was that Jennifer had seen the same grave I had seen next to her. My daughter was unconscious for approximately twelve to fifteen minutes, according to my calculations. When I found her in bed, from the looks of her, I would say she had already been unconscious for approximately five to seven minutes; the rest of the time is the time it took for the staff to get there and revive her. Nobody can be unconscious for twelve to fifteen minutes without having any brain damage. Only by the grace of God and the angels who held could Jennifer have been brought back to me.

The first person I told about this was my mom, Sister Clarissa, who had been a nun in a convent at the time for twelve years. After telling my mom this story, she was impressed but not surprised. I said, "What do you mean?"

She said, "Mark, Jennifer has been chosen to reveal what has happened."

Well, after a long conversation (which they sometimes are with my mom), I was trying to make some sense out of this. But as Mom says, "Why try? It is in God's hands." Well, it takes a long time to grasp this concept, especially when you are a man. When you are the father of a little girl, you take on the responsibility to protect her and take care of her even, or especially, if she has problems, physical or otherwise. But when something like this happens, you find yourself at a loss for words—and sometimes at a loss for direction. You feel like you are losing your grip and don't know what to do or where to turn.

After listening to my mom over the years since I was a young lad, I finally came to this conclusion: no matter how strong you think you are or whether you think you can handle a situation or not, remember that there is a higher-up to let you know that God is in control.

At that time, I made my decision. I said, "God, I leave this in your hands." After Jennifer's story, I don't fear death anymore, and nor does

Jennifer. We just live the best life we can and leave it up to God to do the rest. And to tell you the truth, that puts comfort in my life.

A parent is always conflicted when it comes to his or her child. It had taken Jennifer ten years to tell me her story, but when she did, everything I had seen or felt on the day of her back surgery fell into place. I was actually relieved to know that God is in charge and that we can handle our challenges, no matter how hard, especially when it comes to our children.

Chapter 10

Miss Independent

During the time Jennifer was living with me, we were doing things, going places, dealing with her doctor visits, and so forth. But one thing I noticed was that Jennifer was becoming a young woman, and so were her friends. When Jennifer's friends came over, they were talking about boyfriends and moving out of their homes. Well, that intrigued Jennifer, and she began talking to me about living on her own and being independent.

Well, needless to say, the thought of her being out there on her own scared me to death. There was no way I was going to let my daughter go out on her own without a major plan. So we started talking about options. I took my time with it, hoping she would change her mind, but she was adamant. It was not that she didn't like living with me, which I thought at first; she just wanted to know what she could do on her own.

We finally found an option, and it was the only one I felt good about. We checked into assisted living with twenty-four-hour nursing. We met the staff at a nearby facility, and I have to say, I was impressed. It was a beautiful facility—one of the best in the country. Eighty other people were living there. I felt very comfortable with this, and so did Jennifer, but there was a two-year waiting list, so we waited. Two years went by, and one day we got the call; her room was ready. So we moved her in. It went well until the first night I had to leave her; that was worse that leaving her on the first day of kindergarten. But we made it, and she is still there today. We see each other every week; of course, she lives only twenty minutes away. She still sees doctors all the time and will for the rest of her life. But Jennifer takes it in stride. She doesn't always like it, but she accepts it, because that is who she is.

Jennifer always wanted to be like her friends. Her friends began getting married in their early twenties and starting their own families. Jennifer had always wanted to do that; she talked to me a lot about all this, saying to me, "I can't wait until I get married and have kids."

I tried to stay positive with her, saying, "Sure, honey, maybe someday you will." But I knew different deep down inside. I even talked to her doctor about her ever having kids. His heavy recommendation was that she shouldn't. I asked why, and he told me that she wouldn't survive it and her child might not make it either. Once again, my heart broke for her—and for me, as I had learned I would never be a grandpa. But that's okay; I don't want to jeopardize Jennifer's life just so I can have a grandchild.

I talked with Jennifer about this, and it was a long talk. Even today we still mention it, but she understands. I always said to her, "I don't mind if you have a boyfriend as long as he is your age and very nice to you and I approve." I know most girls just get boyfriends and find out about them for themselves, and that's okay, but my situation is much different, as my daughter is in a vulnerable situation. She wasn't usually happy with this, but I'm her dad. I learned to try to keep this quiet with her, but I'm always watching, and she knows it. I guess I was sometimes overprotective.

After a little time went on, Jennifer decided that if the marriage thing wasn't in the cards, she would try a second time at college downtown. So we both went to visit the college and talk with the administrators, and we got her all signed up. Except this time I couldn't take her there. She started classes, taking a special wheelchair-accessible bus to and from school. I was extremely nervous about this and her being downtown, so we did a dry run and I saw exactly where she was going to be let off—right in front of the school. After a few times of doing this, Jennifer was comfortable with it, and she did well with this for quite a while.

Eventually, I found out Jennifer's other hip was causing her major pain. I asked how long this had been going on, and she said, "For a while now, but I didn't want to say anything because I love school and didn't want you to worry, but the pain is too much to handle." So we saw her doctor, and he said her other hip had to come out, as it was worse than the other one had been. Wouldn't you know it; she had to leave school again for another hip operation. I prepared myself for this, and she did too.

Jennifer was admitted into the hospital, and the next day she had the hip operation. Once again, Dr. Choudhury did a great job. When he was finished, he came out and explained everything he had done. He felt very good about the operation. It does seem a little strange with Jennifer having no hip bones, but since she is never going to walk and is in her chair, this is much more comfortable for her. And you sure can't tell; I don't think Jennifer can even feel the difference.

Jennifer stayed in the hospital for about a week after the surgery, and I visited her every day. It looked like everything was going well. Jennifer stayed on her back the whole time. When I went in to see her one day, I said, "Let's put you on your side."

She said, "I'm okay." But I knew she was in pain.

Jennifer does not like being moved, and I knew she was tired of all the hospitals. So I asked the nurse, "Shouldn't we be putting Jennifer on her side?"

She said, "We tried, but she doesn't want to; she won't let us."

"Why?" I asked.

"Because Jennifer is over eighteen, an adult."

"What?"

"We have to do what they ask."

Jennifer was on her back for two to three days, and I didn't think much about it at first. I should have just turned her on her side and told her to listen to the doctor and staff, but she was in a lot of pain, and I felt very bad for her. But my decision not to do this would have dire consequences that started in the hospital.

Dr. Choudhury gave the okay for Jennifer to go home, and we were glad. But we didn't know at first Jennifer had a very small bedsore near the base of her spine. When she got home to her place, they got her settled in bed. She still had some pain in her hip, but it was getting better. However, the real pain and problem was about to begin.

Jennifer complained about her lower back. When the staff checked it out, they found her bedsore, which had gotten a little worse. The nurses were taking care of it, but it seemed to be getting worse. Her doctor at the facility she lived in saw it and gave her a prescription to help heal it. About another week went by, and Jennifer was feeling worse than ever. Her bedsore had grown bigger. The problem with bedsores is that they grow quickly. They are unlike any other wound, and they are very dangerous. I know, because Jennifer was put in the hospital for hers. And it was an emergency, because by the time I got there right after receiving her call, she was in such a state that she could hardly talk or see me. I was scared to death for her. They pumped her full of heavy antibiotics. There we were, about two weeks out of surgery, and we were back in the hospital for something even worse. Jennifer was in the hospital for weeks; I thought I was going to lose my baby.

We were working with a specialist who performed operations on bedsores. This sore got big made its way down to the bone. Bedsores are very difficult to close up—if they even can be. Jennifer's specialist tried several times but could not get the sore to close.

This particular specialist was not doing a very good job and did not have a good bedside manner, so we switched to a new one, and he seemed to do better. After he got the sore under control, Jennifer started to feel a little better, but this took about three months. Even after being home and being taken care of by her nurses daily, this bedsore, which had started very tiny, grew to a 2"×3" sore that took two years to finally heal completely. These kinds of sores have to heal from inside out and cannot be sown up. Jennifer now has no problem with it when we put her on her side. She also sleeps on a special air bed now. We have not had a problem with bedsores since this one. We all watch her even closer now, and she also works to make sure this won't happen to her again.

Chapter 11

As Life Goes On

There are times when you think you can't go on in life, but as life provides the next day, we get through it. It is always a day-by-day process. Most people, if they were put in Jennifer's position and had to go through everything she has gone through in her life, would want to say, "I just can't do any more." But not Jennifer; despite everything she has gone through, in past, present, and future, she continues to go on every day with a strong attitude. She just loves life; every day is a gift for her, and who could know that better than Jennifer after the experience she went through and still remembers today. All Jennifer ever wanted was just to be as normal as possible.

The school thing had been interrupted several times, so Jennifer began to think about getting a job. When she mentioned this to me, I said, "A job"?

"Why not?" she said. And so we began our new job adventure, figuring out what she could do and wanted to do. After a long deliberation, she decided that she liked computers and always had.

Jennifer had always wanted to make herself useful to both others and herself. But as we looked into jobs, we found ourselves with a new problem. The facility Jennifer lives in costs a lot of money, and that cost is covered by Medicare. Because of the Medicare coverage, Jennifer's hands are tied regarding work. She cannot earn an income; otherwise, her

Medicare will be cut off, and we can't afford for that to happen. So we tried to find something for Jennifer, because she needed to stay busy.

As I was talking with my youngest sister, who happens to work at a hospital—and has worked there for years—we came to a very logical and easy solution.

I asked Jennifer, "How would you like to volunteer at the hospital your aunt works at?"

You would have thought I had just given her a million dollars. She lit up and said, "Yes, of course, I would love to!"

"You will be meeting lots of new people, getting out of the house during the day, and you will be with your aunt," I said.

She cried a little but was very excited; she couldn't wait to start. We set up the job with the hospital and arranged transportation, and she got started. You should have seen her face; she was all proud and happy, which I knew she would be. As time went on, she loved it; everybody at the hospital got to know Jennifer and absolutely loved her and loved to have her there. She felt very important, because she *was* very important. She felt she was accomplishing something, and I was very proud of her.

I think the thing Jennifer loved best about her newfound position was that she got to work with her aunt Mary Anne. Jennifer loves her family; she always enjoys being with them, whether we go out, have picnics, or our big family just goes to see Jennifer at her place on holidays and other occasions. And she is very close to all sixteen of her cousins, especially her cousin Derek, my brother's boy, who was mentioned early on in this book. They grew up together and are almost exactly the same age.

I was surely glad to see Jennifer happy with her job. She would talk about it with her friends; some of them were working, and some weren't. By now some of her friends were having babies and marrying. Jennifer would tell me about this, and I would just say to her, "Don't worry about it," and "It's no big deal," but deep down, she knew. She always tried to keep a positive attitude, though. And this new adventure really helped her. My sister kept in touch with me all the time about how Jennifer was doing at the hospital; she absolutely loved having her there. And the good thing about volunteering for Jennifer was that she could make her own hours, which she did—the more the better for her.

For about eight months, things went pretty well for her. She loved her job with her aunt and didn't need any surgeries for some time. I think we finally had a break.

But this break was short-lived. One day while her caretaker was getting her ready, her leg accidentally got bent too much and was fractured. (One has to be very careful with patients with arthrogryposis; their bones are a lot smaller and more brittle than other people's.) The injury was not extremely serious, but it was enough to get taken care of. She had to quit her volunteer job for a while; she was really sad about that. About four months passed, and she was feeling better. She was still undergoing therapy, but she got to go back to her volunteer job with her aunt.

Again things were all right for about a year, and then Jennifer developed kidney stones. If you have had them, you know what I mean when I say that they are very painful (I know). The doctors figured out a way to remove them gently, but it took about four months to get them to totally disappear. When they finally went away, she didn't go back to work immediately. Sometimes people start thinking *What is the use?* But my daughter didn't give up. Now we take care of the doctor visits, and when she is ready to go back, she will know. Besides, the cost of her bus transportation has gone up a lot; now I will have to pay for her to volunteer when she decides to start up again. For now she is just enjoying herself whenever she can, and that is good enough for me.

Chapter 12

My Life with Jennifer

Life does throw us a lot of curves over the years, and when my Jennifer was born, life threw me a curve unlike any other. I was so proud to be a dad and scared to death as to what to do next. I was a kid at twenty-three years old, and I grew up overnight. Now I have something in my life more important than me—my Jennifer—and I am going to continue to do my best not to disappoint her.

In the Bible, there is a section in which St. Christopher carries the three-year-old baby Jesus on his shoulders through a raging storm in very deep waters. Now three-year-olds don't weigh that much, but St. Christopher kept saying to Jesus, "How does a baby of three keep getting heavier and heavier?" But he made sure he never dropped him. No matter what obstacle was in his way, he made it. Sometimes that's how I have felt in life; the weight of the world was on my shoulders and kept on getting heavier, but I made a promise to my daughter: "I will never drop you."

My life with Jennifer has been absolutely rewarding, through all the good times and the rough times. And when bad things happened to my child year after year, I tried every day not to show weakness; my Jennifer had to see me as her rock that she could always depend on. Jennifer has endured a lot in her life; it's more than I or anybody can comprehend.

I often felt Jennifer missed out on much of life, and I often felt bad for her; I can't even explain it. But I tried to do all I could to make her feel as normal as possible in everything we did. Jennifer changed my life more than she knows; she was a big inspiration, and she gave me patience to deal with life during many moments when I most needed it.

Other inspirations in my life were my mom, Sr. Clarissa. She helped me pull through during a lot of hard times, and sometimes I didn't always agree with her, but she was there nonetheless.

A couple of years ago, I saw a man named Joel Osteen on TV one Sunday morning. Now I am not into TV preachers, but the first time I saw and heard him, I was intrigued and hooked; now watching his show is a ritual for me every Sunday. It seems that every Sunday when he delivers his sermon, it always feels as though he is talking to me directly, and each Sunday gets better. It makes me feel as though everything is going to be all right. His show has put a lot of things in perspective in my life; and through that show, I have made a breakthrough into continuing on.

As human beings, we all have a fear of death, the unknown; we fret over where we will go and what will happen to us. But sometimes I think we get a second chance—not only for the person who was about to leave us, but for all to know about that second chance. My daughter got her second chance at life when the angels brought her back to me. But I also think they did so for me, to give me my second chance in life, to allow me to know that there is a much higher God that is in control, and to let me know that everything is okay and not to fall apart. He is there for us, and we need to have faith in him. After Jennifer's experience with the angels, I really don't fear death anymore, because I know God has me in the palm of his hand, and he does all who believe and have faith in him.

After hearing Jennifer's story, I feel not only at ease but also at peace, and most of all, I feel completely blessed. I can't believe one little girl could put so much faith in me. Jennifer is now twenty-nine years old and the absolute love of my life. She always has been and always will be. God has sent me an angel from heaven to take care of her life, and I promised I would, both to God and to my little girl. And I feel completely blessed every day for having been able to know her. It has not always been easy, but it has been rewarding knowing that I have been chosen for this.

There is no doubt in my mind as to what I experienced and what Jennifer saw and where she was that day in the hospital. I know those angels saved my daughter's life and brought her back to me, and I believe that they wanted me to know this and that they wanted to help bring peace into my life. That day is one I will never forget, knowing that the angels saved my daughter. There is another angel that was sent to me to save my life, and she doesn't even know it; that angel is my daughter, my Jennifer.

I don't know what the future holds for Jennifer; all we can do is take life day by day. I would like to think that things will get better, but I leave it in God's hands. He counts on me, his disciple, to take care of his angel; I hope I have not failed him or Jennifer.

We still continue to see doctors on a regular basis. The older Jennifer gets, the more often it seems things come up that need to be taken care of. But I know Dr. Choudhury will always be there for her.

Jennifer has accepted her way of life above and beyond human capacity, and that makes me proud and sad at the same time. I am very proud of my angel, and I hope she knows the good she has brought to my life. She has made me the man I am.

I love you.

Jennifer today

About the Author

Mark was born February 3, 1959. He is the oldest of 5 brothers and 2 sisters, and had great parents. They were a catholic middle class family. Dad, an immigrant from Germany, was a supervisor at a plant and worked hard for his family. Mom was a wonderful homemaker and took great care of her family. They live in a middle class neighborhood in Bridgetown, Ohio. Mark grew up with good family values and good friends in his neighborhood. All his brothers and sisters are very close and still live close to each other. When they were young, sometimes they fight and say things like, "I wish I was the only child", but as young adults they start realizing what they have in each other, as you get older and it's great. And Mark wouldn't have it any other way. God blessed him with a great family. As a student in school he was average and was a little wild, but got through it. At age 19 he quit his job and sold everything, bought a nice car and did some traveling and saw other parts of this country. It was a great time in his life. When he finally came back home, he got back with his girlfriend and 1-½ years later got married. And two years later they had their little girl Jennifer. Sixteen years later, unfortunately, their marriage didn't last. And seventeen years later still did not get remarried, and doesn't know if he ever will. But Jennifer remains his priority in his & her life.

Jennifer is the oldest of 17 grandchildren.

www.ingramcontent.com/pod-product-compliance
Ingram Content Group UK Ltd.
Pitfield, Milton Keynes, MK11 3LW, UK
UKHW041917190726
13854UKWH00003B/1287

9 781449 788162